THIS BOOK BELONGS TO:

_____

THE CHRISTMAS SEASON IS THE MOST MAGICAL TIME OF THE YEAR! OR AT LEAST IT SHOULD BE; WITH ALL OF THE HUSTLE OF BUYING AND WRAPPING CHRISTMAS GIFTS, PLANNING A PERFECT CHRISTMAS DINNER MENU FOR THE WHOLE FAMILY, AND CLOSING THE LAST DEAL AT THE OFFICE, THIS TIME OF YEAR CAN GET QUITE STRESSFUL. SO IT'S IMPORTANT TO REFLECT ON THIS BEAUTIFUL SEASON AND REMIND OURSELVES THAT THIS IS A TIME OF JOY AND LAUGHTER.

I'VE GOT YOU COVERED WITH THE 200 CHRISTMAS WOULD YOU RATHER QUESTIONS, THAT WILL BRING A SMILE TO THE FACE OF EVERY MEMBER OF YOUR FAMILY. SO, WHEN CHRISTMAS TIME COMES, GATHER WITH THE KIDS, GRAB THIS LITTLE BOOK AND SEE IF YOU CAN GET A "HO-HO-HO" OUT OF THEM. I HOPE THIS BOOK WILL HELP YOU TO CELEBRATE THIS JOYFUL TIME AND SPARKLE THE TRUE MAGIC OF THIS CHRISTMAS SEASON.

WOULD YOU RATHER HAVE A SNOWBALL FIGHT WITH SANTA
OR
BUILD A SNOWMAN WITH THE ELVES?

WOULD YOU RATHER GET SOCKS FOR CHRISTMAS
OR
GET UNDERWEAR FOR CHRISTMAS?

WOULD YOU RATHER HAVE
RUDOLPH'S GLOWING NOSE FOR A
WEEK
OR SANTA'S BEARD FOR A
MONTH?

WOULD YOU RATHER EAT ONLY
CANDY CANES FOR A DAY
OR
DRINK ONLY HOT CHOCOLATE
FOR A DAY?

WOULD YOU RATHER LIVE IN A
SNOW GLOBE
OR
IN A GINGERBREAD HOUSE?

WOULD YOU RATHER SING JINGLE
BELLS EVERY TIME YOU SPEAK
OR
DANCE WHENEVER YOU HEAR
MUSIC?

WOULD YOU RATHER BE A CHRISTMAS ELF FOR A DAY
OR
A REINDEER FOR A DAY?

WOULD YOU RATHER WRAP PRESENTS FOR 8 HOURS STRAIGHT OR
UNTANGLE CHRISTMAS LIGHTS FOR 4 HOURS?

WOULD YOU RATHER HAVE A
CHRISTMAS TREE THAT
DECORATES ITSELF
OR
STOCKINGS THAT FILL
THEMSELVES UP?

WOULD YOU RATHER SPEND
A DAY SLEDDING
OR
BUILDING SNOW FORTS?

WOULD YOU RATHER HAVE YOUR TONGUE STUCK TO A FROZEN POLE
OR
SLIDE DOWN A HILL WITH NO SLED?

WOULD YOU RATHER BE IN CHARGE OF MAKING SNOW
OR
CONTROLLING THE WINTER WIND?

WOULD YOU RATHER HAVE A
SNOW DAY EVERY DAY
OR
CHRISTMAS EVERY MONTH?

WOULD YOU RATHER ONLY BE
ABLE TO WHISPER "HO! HO! HO!"
EVERY TIME YOU SPEAK
OR
HAVE JINGLE BELLS ON YOUR
SHOES THAT RING WHENEVER YOU
WALK?

WOULD YOU RATHER GET A VISIT
FROM FROSTY THE SNOWMAN
OR
THE GRINCH ON CHRISTMAS
MORNING?

WOULD YOU RATHER EAT A
WHOLE FRUITCAKE BY YOURSELF
OR
HAVE TO WEAR A CHRISTMAS
SWEATER EVERY DAY FOR A
YEAR?

WOULD YOU RATHER RIDE IN
SANTA'S SLEIGH
OR
DANCE AT THE NORTH POLE
WITH THE ELVES?

WOULD YOU RATHER BE ABLE TO
CREATE SNOWFLAKES BY BLOWING
ON YOUR HANDS
OR
WARM UP ANYTHING INSTANTLY
BY TOUCHING IT?

WOULD YOU RATHER HAVE A PET
PENGUIN
OR
A PET POLAR BEAR?

WOULD YOU RATHER HAVE CANDY
CANE FINGERS
OR
SNOWBALL HANDS?

WOULD YOU RATHER HAVE SNOW
FOR HAIR
OR
CANDY CANES FOR TEETH?

WOULD YOU RATHER SNEEZE OUT
TINSEL
OR
COUGH UP CHRISTMAS
ORNAMENTS?

WOULD YOU RATHER HAVE ELF
EARS THAT WIGGLE WHEN YOU'RE
EXCITED

OR

A REINDEER TAIL THAT GLOWS IN
THE DARK?

WOULD YOU RATHER SLIDE DOWN A
GIANT CANDY CANE

OR

JUMP ON A TRAMPOLINE MADE OF
FRUITCAKE?

WOULD YOU RATHER HAVE YOUR
SWEAT SMELL LIKE GINGERBREAD
OR
YOUR BURPS SOUND LIKE JINGLE
BELLS?

WOULD YOU RATHER BATHE IN A
TUB FULL OF EGGNOG
OR
BRUSH YOUR TEETH WITH MINTY
SNOW PASTE?

WOULD YOU RATHER BE TICKLED
BY A CHRISTMAS TREE EVERY
MORNING
OR
HAVE MISTLETOE GROW FROM
YOUR NOSE?

WOULD YOU RATHER HAVE TO EAT
A SNOWMAN'S CARROT NOSE
OR
DRINK MELTED SNOWMAN WATER?

WOULD YOU RATHER RIDE A
ROLLER COASTER MADE OF
RIBBON
OR
BE TRAPPED IN A BUBBLE OF
FLOATING CHRISTMAS BAUBLE?

WOULD YOU RATHER HAVE ICICLES
HANGING FROM YOUR NOSTRILS
OR
SNOWFLAKES CONSTANTLY
FALLING FROM YOUR EARS?

WOULD YOU RATHER ALWAYS
WALK LEAVING STICKY
GINGERBREAD FOOTPRINTS
OR HAVE CANDY WRAPPERS FALL
OUT OF YOUR POCKETS EVERY
TIME YOU RUN?

WOULD YOU RATHER HAVE
CHRISTMAS WRAPPING PAPER FOR
SKIN
OR
ORNAMENTS FOR EYES?

WOULD YOU RATHER HAVE TO
GULP DOWN A MUG OF GRAVY
OR
CHEW ON A CHRISTMAS
STOCKING?

WOULD YOU RATHER FIND OUT
THAT YOUR BEST FRIEND IS AN
UNDERCOVER ELF
OR
THAT YOUR TEACHER TURNS INTO A
SNOWMAN ON WEEKENDS?

WOULD YOU RATHER GET STUCK
IN A GIANT JELLO SNOW GLOBE
OR
HAVE EVERY SNOWFLAKE THAT
TOUCHES YOU TURN INTO
POPCORN?

WOULD YOU RATHER BLOW BUBBLE
GUM BUBBLES FILLED WITH
GLITTER
OR
SNEEZE OUT CONFETTI?

WOULD YOU RATHER HAVE YOUR
FINGERS ALWAYS SMELL LIKE
ROASTED CHESTNUTS
OR
YOUR HAIR CONSTANTLY SPARKLE
LIKE CHRISTMAS LIGHTS?

WOULD YOU RATHER BE CHASED BY
A GIANT SNOWBALL
OR
HAVE TO RACE A RUNAWAY SLED
DOWNHILL?

WOULD YOU RATHER FIND COAL-
FLAVORED CANDY IN YOUR
STOCKING

OR

GET A PRESENT THAT FARTS
CHRISTMAS CAROLS?

WOULD YOU RATHER EAT A
SPAGHETTI SNOWBALL

OR

LICK A CANDY-COATED ICICLE?

WOULD YOU RATHER HAVE YOUR NOSE RUN WITH GREEN HOLIDAY GLITTER

OR

SNEEZE OUT MINI CHRISTMAS BAUBLES?

WOULD YOU RATHER FIND SANTA'S BEARD HAIRS IN YOUR HOT CHOCOLATE

OR

AN ELF'S HAT IN YOUR SOUP?

WOULD YOU RATHER CLEAN UP
AFTER THE REINDEER'S
"PRESENTS" IN YOUR YARD
OR
HAVE A SNOWMAN THAT MELTS
INTO A PUDDLE OF GRAVY?

WOULD YOU RATHER HAVE
EARWAX THAT TASTES LIKE
CANDY CANES
OR
TOENAILS THAT SMELL LIKE
ROASTED TURKEY?

WOULD YOU RATHER HAVE
CHRISTMAS TREES GROW OUT OF
YOUR ARMPITS
OR
SNOWFLAKES THAT FORM EVERY
TIME YOU DROOL?

WOULD YOU RATHER DRINK A CUP
OF MELTED SNOWMAN SWEAT
OR
EAT COOKIES BAKED BY THE
GRINCH WITH HIS FEET?

WOULD YOU RATHER SLIDE DOWN
A HILL COVERED IN MASHED
POTATOES
OR
JUMP INTO A POOL FILLED WITH
CRANBERRY SAUCE?

WOULD YOU RATHER HAVE TO
LICK A FROZEN POLE EVERY
MORNING
OR
BITE INTO A COLD, FROSTY
WORM?

WOULD YOU RATHER HAVE TO
LICK A FROZEN POLE EVERY
MORNING
OR
BITE INTO A COLD, FROSTY
WORM?

WOULD YOU RATHER USE A
SNOWBALL MADE FROM REINDEER
SPIT IN A SNOWBALL FIGHT
OR
BUILD A SNOWMAN USING MASHED
BRUSSELS SPROUTS?

WOULD YOU RATHER SWEAT
MAPLE SYRUP
OR
HAVE YOUR HICCUPS SOUND LIKE
SANTA'S BELLY LAUGH?

WOULD YOU RATHER HAVE
CHRISTMAS TINSEL
FOR
DENTAL FLOSS OR USE MISTLETOE
AS TOILET PAPER?

WOULD YOU RATHER EAT A
GINGERBREAD HOUSE COVERED IN
MUSTARD
OR
DRINK A HOT CHOCOLATE MIXED
WITH PICKLES?

WOULD YOU RATHER BLOW YOUR
NOSE WITH SANDPAPER-WRAPPED
PRESENTS
OR
USE PINE NEEDLES AS
TOOTHPICKS?

WOULD YOU RATHER FIND OUT THAT SNOWFLAKES ARE ACTUALLY FROZEN SNEEZES FROM THE NORTH POLE OR THAT CANDY CANES ARE MADE FROM SANTA'S RECYCLED CANDY?

WOULD YOU RATHER HAVE A CHRISTMAS TURKEY THAT SQUAWKS EVERY TIME YOU TRY TO CARVE IT OR PUDDING THAT WRIGGLES AWAY FROM YOUR SPOON?

WOULD YOU RATHER BE TICKLED BY A TREE WITH COLD, SLIMY BRANCHES
OR HUGGED BY A SNOWMAN WITH ARMS MADE OF WET SPAGHETTI?

WOULD YOU RATHER STEP ON CRUNCHY ORNAMENTS EVERY TIME YOU WALK
OR
LEAVE A TRAIL OF STICKY CANDY CANE RESIDUE BEHIND YOU?

WOULD YOU RATHER BE TRAPPED IN A SNOW GLOBE FILLED WITH CLAM CHOWDER
OR
SLED DOWN A HILL OF COLD SPAGHETTI?

WOULD YOU RATHER RECEIVE A GIFT THAT'S ALIVE AND SLIMY
OR
UNWRAP A BOX THAT CONSTANTLY EMITS THE SMELL OF STINKY CHEESE?

WOULD YOU RATHER FLY AROUND THE WORLD ON SANTA'S SLEIGH

OR

GO ON A CRUISE WITH FROSTY THE SNOWMAN AS THE CAPTAIN?

WOULD YOU RATHER GET LOST IN A GIANT CHRISTMAS MAZE MADE OF CANDY CANES

OR

SLIDE ENDLESSLY ON A GLOBAL ICY BANANA PEEL?

WOULD YOU RATHER TAKE A WINTER VACATION INSIDE A SNOW GLOBE
OR
IN A GIANT CHRISTMAS STOCKING?

WOULD YOU RATHER GO SKIING WITH A GROUP OF GIGGLING GINGERBREAD MEN
OR
ICE SKATING WITH DANCING REINDEER?

WOULD YOU RATHER VISIT THE NORTH POLE BUT ONLY BE ALLOWED TO PACK SWIMSUITS OR GO TO THE BEACH AND ONLY PACK SNOW BOOTS AND WOOLLY MITTENS?

WOULD YOU RATHER HAVE A SNOWBALL FIGHT ATOP THE EIFFEL TOWER
OR
BUILD A SNOWMAN ON THE GREAT WALL OF CHINA?

WOULD YOU RATHER TRAVEL ON A TRAIN THAT ONLY SERVES BRUSSELS SPROUTS FLAVORED HOT CHOCOLATE OR FLY ON A PLANE WHERE THE IN-FLIGHT MOVIE IS JUST RUDOLPH'S NOSE BLINKING?

WOULD YOU RATHER STAY AT A HOTEL WHERE THE BELLBOY IS AN ELF
OR
EAT AT A RESTAURANT WHERE ALL THE WAITERS ARE SNOWMEN?

WOULD YOU RATHER GO ON A ROAD TRIP WITH THE GRINCH COMPLAINING ABOUT THE MUSIC OR WITH SANTA CLAUS ALWAYS STOPPING FOR COOKIES?

WOULD YOU RATHER RIDE A ROLLER COASTER WITH SANTA'S REINDEER

OR

GO ON A MERRY-GO-ROUND OF SPINNING CHRISTMAS TREES?

WOULD YOU RATHER GO CAMPING IN A TENT MADE OF WRAPPING PAPER

OR

SLEEP IN A SNOW FORT AT THE ICE HOTEL?

WOULD YOU RATHER SAIL ON A SHIP WITH SAILS MADE OF GIANT ELF HATS

OR

IN A SUBMARINE SHAPED LIKE A MASSIVE CHRISTMAS BAUBLE?

WOULD YOU RATHER CLIMB A MOUNTAIN THAT CONSTANTLY PLAYS "JINGLE BELLS"
OR
ZIPLINE THROUGH A FOREST OF TWINKLING CHRISTMAS LIGHTS?

WOULD YOU RATHER DISCOVER AN ISLAND WHERE SAND LOOKS LIKE SUGAR AND WAVES ARE MADE OF EGGNOG OR A DESERT WHERE CACTI ARE CANDY CANES AND TUMBLEWEEDS ARE TINSEL?

WOULD YOU RATHER HIKE WITH
PENGUINS WEARING FESTIVE
SWEATERS
OR
GO ON A SAFARI TO SPOT
CHRISTMAS TREES IN THE WILD?

WOULD YOU RATHER GO DEEP-SEA
DIVING TO FIND SANTA'S LOST
PRESENTS
OR EXPLORE A JUNGLE WITH
CANDY CANE VINES AND
CHOCOLATE RIVERS?

WOULD YOU RATHER TAKE A HOT AIR BALLOON RIDE POWERED BY HOLIDAY WISHES
OR
RIDE A BIKE WITH CANDY CANE WHEELS?

WOULD YOU RATHER EXPLORE A CAVE FILLED WITH HOLIDAY BATS WEARING SANTA HATS OR FIND A WATERFALL THAT POURS GLITTERING HOLIDAY CHEER?

WOULD YOU RATHER BACKPACK ACROSS A COUNTRY WHERE IT SNOWS MARSHMALLOWS OR CROSS A CONTINENT WHERE THE RAIN IS SPARKLING APPLE CIDER?

WOULD YOU RATHER HAVE A MAP THAT SHOWS THE LOCATION OF HIDDEN CHRISTMAS PRESENTS WORLDWIDE OR A COMPASS THAT ALWAYS POINTS TO THE NEAREST HOLIDAY FEAST?

WOULD YOU RATHER RECEIVE A
PET UNICORN THAT GRANTS
WISHES
OR
A MAGIC CARPET THAT CAN FLY
ANYWHERE IN THE WORLD?

WOULD YOU RATHER GET THE
ABILITY TO SPEAK TO ANIMALS
OR
RECEIVE A LIFETIME SUPPLY OF
YOUR FAVORITE CANDY?

WOULD YOU RATHER RECEIVE A MAGIC PEN THAT BRINGS DRAWINGS TO LIFE
OR A BOOK WHERE CHARACTERS STEP OUT AND BECOME REAL FRIENDS?

WOULD YOU RATHER BE GIFTED A DAY WHERE EVERY HOUR IS A SURPRISE ADVENTURE OR A BOX WITH A MYSTERIOUS OBJECT FROM THE FUTURE?

WOULD YOU RATHER RECEIVE A TELESCOPE THAT LETS YOU SEE INTO OTHER GALAXIES OR A PAIR OF GLASSES THAT TRANSLATE EVERY LANGUAGE?

WOULD YOU RATHER BE GIFTED THE SKILL OF PLAYING ANY INSTRUMENT PERFECTLY OR THE ABILITY TO DANCE FLAWLESSLY IN ANY STYLE?

WOULD YOU RATHER GET A MAGIC WARDROBE THAT LEADS TO ANOTHER WORLD OR A REMOTE CONTROL THAT CAN PAUSE, REWIND, OR FAST-FORWARD TIME?

WOULD YOU RATHER RECEIVE A TREEHOUSE THAT CHANGES THEMES DAILY
OR
A TENT THAT TAKES YOU TO A NEW FANTASY WORLD EACH NIGHT?

WOULD YOU RATHER BE GIFTED A POTION THAT LETS YOU CHANGE APPEARANCE AT WILL

OR

SHOES THAT MAKE YOU INVISIBLE?

WOULD YOU RATHER RECEIVE A ROBOT BUTLER

OR

A FRIENDLY GHOST BUDDY WHO TELLS FASCINATING STORIES FROM THE PAST?

WOULD YOU RATHER BE GIFTED A
TIME-TRAVELING WATCH
OR
A MAP THAT SHOWS HIDDEN
TREASURES AROUND THE WORLD?

WOULD YOU RATHER RECEIVE A
MACHINE THAT MAKES ANY FOOD
YOU DESIRE OR A NECKLACE THAT
LETS YOU TALK TO INANIMATE
OBJECTS?

WOULD YOU RATHER GET A DAY WHERE EVERY SINGLE WISH YOU MAKE COMES TRUE OR A YEAR WHERE EVERY DREAM YOU HAVE BECOMES A SHORT MOVIE?

WOULD YOU RATHER BE GIFTED A PET DRAGON
OR
A MAGICAL GARDEN WHERE PLANTS AND FLOWERS CHAT WITH YOU?

WOULD YOU RATHER RECEIVE A JOURNAL WHERE CHARACTERS GIVE ADVICE OR A RADIO THAT PLAYS SONGS FROM DIFFERENT DIMENSIONS?

WOULD YOU RATHER GET A TOY FACTORY THAT DESIGNS TOYS BASED ON YOUR IMAGINATION OR A MAGIC PAINTBRUSH THAT COLORS YOUR WORLD IN NEW WAYS?

WOULD YOU RATHER BE GIFTED ENDLESS PLANE TICKETS TO TRAVEL THE WORLD OR A DIARY THAT LETS YOU EXPERIENCE ANY HISTORICAL EVENT?

WOULD YOU RATHER RECEIVE A ROOM THAT CHANGES INTO ANY ENVIRONMENT YOU WISH OR A CLOUD THAT YOU CAN RIDE ACROSS THE SKIES?

WOULD YOU RATHER BE GIFTED THE KNOWLEDGE OF EVERY BOOK EVER WRITTEN OR A MELODY THAT UPLIFTS ANYONE WHO HEARS IT?

WOULD YOU RATHER RECEIVE A PUZZLE THAT SHOWS YOUR FUTURE WHEN COMPLETED OR A KEY THAT OPENS ANY DOOR IN THE WORLD?

WOULD YOU RATHER RECEIVE A HAT THAT ALLOWS YOU TO THINK LIKE A GENIUS FOR AN HOUR DAILY OR GLOVES THAT LET YOU SCULPT ANYTHING OUT OF THIN AIR?

WOULD YOU RATHER BE GIFTED A MAGIC MIRROR THAT SHOWS ALTERNATE REALITIES OR A DOOR MAT THAT TELEPORTS YOU TO A CHOSEN DESTINATION?

WOULD YOU RATHER RECEIVE A CRYSTAL BALL THAT REVEALS ONE SECRET ABOUT THE UNIVERSE OR A RING THAT LETS YOU HEAR THE THOUGHTS OF TREES AND FLOWERS?

WOULD YOU RATHER BE GIFTED A CHARM THAT ENSURES YOU ALWAYS HAVE PERFECT WEATHER OR A SCARF THAT CHANGES COLOR BASED ON YOUR MOOD?

WOULD YOU RATHER GET A LANTERN THAT HOLDS CAPTURED DREAMS
OR
A BRACELET THAT GIVES YOU THE AGILITY OF A SUPERHERO?

WOULD YOU RATHER RECEIVE A PILLOW THAT GUARANTEES THE SWEETEST DREAMS OR A CLOCK THAT GIVES YOU AN EXTRA HOUR IN THE DAY?

WOULD YOU RATHER RECEIVE A MUG THAT FILLS WITH ANY DRINK YOU THINK OF

OR

AN ENDLESS STORYBOOK THAT NEVER REPEATS A TALE?

WOULD YOU RATHER BE GIFTED A COIN THAT ALWAYS LANDS ON WHAT'S BEST FOR YOU OR A COMPASS THAT POINTS TO WHATEVER YOU'RE SEEKING?

WOULD YOU RATHER GET A BASKET OF FRUITS FROM FAIRY TALES (LIKE GOLDEN APPLES)
OR
A SPICE RACK WITH MAGICAL SEASONINGS?

WOULD YOU RATHER BE GIFTED A FEATHER THAT LETS YOU FLOAT
OR
A PEBBLE THAT GROUNDS YOU NO MATTER HOW CHAOTIC THINGS GET?

WOULD YOU RATHER RECEIVE A
CAMERA THAT CAPTURES HiDDEN
MAGICAL MOMENTS
OR
A MUSIC BOX THAT PLAYS TUNES
FROM FORGOTTEN WORLDS?

WOULD YOU RATHER GET A
POCKET-SiZED SUN FOR ENDLESS
LiGHT
OR
A MiNiATURE MOON TO LULL YOU
TO SLEEP?

WOULD YOU RATHER BE GIFTED A
QUILL THAT WRITES STORIES AS
YOU DREAM THEM
OR
A CANVAS THAT PAINTS ITSELF
BASED ON YOUR DAY?

WOULD YOU RATHER RECEIVE A
BOAT THAT SAILS
ON
CLOUDS OR A KITE THAT CAN LIFT
YOU INTO THE SKY?

WOULD YOU RATHER BE GIFTED A
SEED THAT GROWS A NEW SURPRISE
PLANT MONTHLY
OR
A FOUNTAIN THAT SPROUTS STORIES
INSTEAD OF WATER?

WOULD YOU RATHER GET A
LOCKET THAT SHOWS PICTURES
FROM THE PAST
OR
A WATCH THAT HINTS AT POSSIBLE
FUTURES?

WOULD YOU RATHER RECEIVE A TAPESTRY THAT DEPICTS YOUR GRANDEST ADVENTURES
OR
A MOSAIC THAT REFLECTS YOUR MOST HEARTFELT EMOTIONS?

WOULD YOU RATHER BE GIFTED A CANDLE THAT BURNS WITH SCENTS OF PLACES YOU'VE NEVER BEEN OR A BELL THAT RINGS WITH ECHOES FROM HISTORY?

WOULD YOU RATHER GET A CAPE THAT WRAPS YOU IN COURAGE
OR
A BELT THAT ENDOWS BOUNDLESS ENERGY?

WOULD YOU RATHER RECEIVE A DECK OF CARDS, EACH REVEALING A UNIQUE SKILL WHEN DRAWN, OR A DICE THAT PREDICTS YOUR LUCK FOR THE DAY?

WOULD YOU RATHER HAVE A SNOWBALL FIGHT WITH YOUR FAMILY OR BUILD THE BIGGEST SNOW FORT IN THE NEIGHBORHOOD TOGETHER?

WOULD YOU RATHER FIND OUT YOUR GRANDMA IS SECRETLY MRS. CLAUS OR THAT YOUR UNCLE HELPS SANTA DESIGN TOYS AT THE NORTH POLE?

WOULD YOU RATHER BAKE AND DECORATE CHRISTMAS COOKIES WITH YOUR SIBLINGS OR GO CAROLING AROUND THE NEIGHBORHOOD WITH YOUR COUSINS?

WOULD YOU RATHER SPEND CHRISTMAS MORNING WITH YOUR FAMILY IN A COZY CABIN IN THE MOUNTAINS OR ON A SUNNY BEACH WITH A SNOWY PALM TREE?

WOULD YOU RATHER HAVE A
FAMILY TRADITION OF OPENING
PRESENTS AT MIDNIGHT
OR
WAITING UNTIL THE EVENING OF
CHRISTMAS DAY?

WOULD YOU RATHER SEE YOUR
FAMILY MEMBERS PERFORM A
HOLIDAY PLAY
OR
JOIN THEM IN A FESTIVE DANCE-
OFF?

WOULD YOU RATHER PICK OUT THE
FAMILY CHRISTMAS TREE WITH
EVERYONE IN SUMMER SHORTS
OR
WHILE EVERYONE'S WEARING
WACKY WINTER ONESIES?

WOULD YOU RATHER HAVE YOUR
FAMILY'S PET LEAD SANTA'S
REINDEER
OR BE THE STAR ON TOP OF THE
NORTH POLE'S LARGEST
CHRISTMAS TREE?

WOULD YOU RATHER SPEND A
WINTER EVENING SIPPING COCOA
AND HEARING FAMILY STORIES
OR
GO SLEDDING WITH EVERYONE
UNDER THE NORTHERN LIGHTS?

WOULD YOU RATHER HELP YOUR
PARENTS COOK A HOLIDAY FEAST
FOR A WEEK
OR
DO ALL THE FESTIVE
DECORATIONS IN THE HOUSE?

WOULD YOU RATHER FIND OUT YOUR SIBLING SECRETLY HAS THE POWER TO MAKE IT SNOW OR THAT YOUR BEST FAMILY FRIEND IS ACTUALLY A SNOWMAN IN DISGUISE?

WOULD YOU RATHER HAVE YOUR ENTIRE FAMILY WEAR MATCHING UGLY CHRISTMAS SWEATERS

OR

HAVE EVERYONE WEAR DIFFERENT HOLIDAY HATS?

WOULD YOU RATHER UNWRAP A PRESENT THAT LETS YOUR FAMILY TELEPORT TO ANY HOLIDAY DESTINATION OR ONE THAT FREEZES TIME SO YOU CAN ENJOY LONGER CELEBRATIONS?

WOULD YOU RATHER JOIN YOUR FAMILY IN A GIANT CHRISTMAS-THEMED ESCAPE ROOM

OR

A WINTER WONDERLAND SCAVENGER HUNT?

WOULD YOU RATHER WATCH YOUR FAVORITE HOLIDAY MOVIE WITH YOUR FAMILY IN A SNOW GLOBE CINEMA
OR ON A SCREEN MADE OF TWINKLING STARS?

WOULD YOU RATHER HAVE A FAMILY SNOW SCULPTURE CONTEST OR A FESTIVE TALENT SHOW WHERE EVERYONE SHOWCASES A UNIQUE HOLIDAY SKILL?

WOULD YOU RATHER YOUR FAMILY RECEIVE A LETTER FROM SANTA PRAISING YOUR FESTIVE SPIRIT
OR
GET A SPECIAL VISIT FROM THE ELVES FOR A DAY OF FUN?

WOULD YOU RATHER HAVE A CHRISTMAS WHERE EVERY FAMILY MEMBER'S GIFT TO EACH OTHER WAS A FUN EXPERIENCE OR WHERE EACH GIFT WAS HANDMADE WITH LOVE?

WOULD YOU RATHER SEE YOUR FAMILY'S OLDEST HOLIDAY TRADITIONS FROM THE PAST THROUGH A MAGIC WINDOW OR CREATE NEW ONES THAT WILL LAST FOR CENTURIES?

WOULD YOU RATHER HAVE A HOLIDAY DINNER WHERE EVERY FAMILY MEMBER'S FAVORITE DISH MAGICALLY APPEARS OR WHERE EACH DISH TELLS A STORY FROM FAMILY HISTORY?

WOULD YOU RATHER FIND OUT THAT YOUR BED TURNS INTO A GIANT JELLY SANDWICH EVERY NIGHT OR THAT YOUR PILLOW BECOMES A GIGGLING WATERMELON?

WOULD YOU RATHER HAVE YOUR FAVORITE TOY START SINGING THE MOST ANNOYING SONG NON-STOP OR DISCOVER YOUR SCHOOL BOOKS WHISPERING YOUR SECRETS?

WOULD YOU RATHER REALIZE THAT ALL YOUR CLOTHES HAVE TURNED INTO COSTUMES OF VEGGIES OR THAT YOUR SHOES WON'T STOP MOOING LIKE COWS?

WOULD YOU RATHER WAKE UP TO FIND YOUR HAIR MADE OF SPAGHETTI OR THAT YOUR FINGERS HAVE TURNED INTO WIGGLY GUMMY WORMS?

WOULD YOU RATHER DISCOVER THAT YOUR BATHTUB IS FILLED WITH CHOCOLATE PUDDING (BUT YOU CAN'T EAT IT!) OR THAT YOUR TOOTHBRUSH IS DETERMINED TO BRUSH YOUR TOES INSTEAD OF YOUR TEETH?

WOULD YOU RATHER HAVE YOUR BEDROOM WALLS START SHOWING EMBARRASSING BABY PHOTOS OF YOU OR THAT YOUR FAVORITE SNACK NOW ONLY TALKS BACK INSTEAD OF BEING EDIBLE?

WOULD YOU RATHER FIND OUT
EVERY TIME YOU YAWN, BUBBLES
FLOAT OUT OF YOUR MOUTH
OR
EVERY SNEEZE SOUNDS LIKE A
DUCK QUACKING?

WOULD YOU RATHER HAVE YOUR
BACKPACK START ASKING TRICKY
RIDDLES BEFORE OPENING OR
YOUR LUNCHBOX ONLY SERVING
BROCCOLI-FLAVORED ICE
CREAM?

WOULD YOU RATHER THAT EVERY DRAWING YOU MAKE COMES TO LIFE (AND CRITICIZES YOUR ARTISTIC SKILLS) OR THAT YOUR PETS NOW SPEAK IN A SHAKESPEAREAN MANNER?

WOULD YOU RATHER THAT EVERY VIDEO GAME YOU PLAY STARTS GIVING YOU HOMEWORK TASKS OR THAT YOUR FAVORITE STORYBOOK CHARACTERS COMPLAIN ABOUT THEIR PLOTS?

WOULD YOU RATHER THAT YOUR SHADOWS PLAY MISCHIEVOUS PRANKS
OR THAT YOUR REFLECTION IN THE MIRROR CHALLENGES YOU TO SILLY DANCE-OFFS?

WOULD YOU RATHER FIND OUT THAT EVERY STUFFED TOY IN YOUR ROOM FORMS A COMMITTEE TO DISCUSS BEDTIME HOURS OR THAT YOUR DIARY/JOURNAL NOW GIVES YOU SASSY ADVICE?

WOULD YOU RATHER HAVE EVERY DESSERT YOU TOUCH TURN INTO RAW VEGGIES OR DISCOVER THAT RAIN CLOUDS FOLLOW YOU TO ENSURE YOU GET A SPLASH, EVEN INDOORS?

WOULD YOU RATHER DISCOVER THAT YOUR PENCILS AND PENS HAVE FORMED A UNION AND GONE ON STRIKE OR THAT YOUR BICYCLE PEDALS ARGUE ABOUT WHICH WAY TO GO?

WOULD YOU RATHER THAT YOUR BED INSISTS ON BEDTIME STORIES BEFORE LETTING YOU SLEEP OR YOUR ALARM CLOCK DEMANDS A GOOD MORNING SONG EACH DAY?

WOULD YOU RATHER WAKE UP TO FIND ALL YOUR TOYS SWITCHED ROLES (YOUR TOY CAR IS NOW A TEDDY BEAR AND VICE VERSA) OR THAT YOUR BEDROOM DECOR IS THEMED AROUND THE ONE COLOR YOU DISLIKE?

WOULD YOU RATHER FIND OUT THAT YOUR SOCKS ARE PLOTTING AN ESCAPE PLAN OR THAT YOUR FAVORITE HAT NOW THINKS IT'S A CROWN AND DEMANDS RESPECT?

WOULD YOU RATHER HAVE YOUR SCHOOL'S MASCOT FOLLOW YOU AROUND NARRATING YOUR DAY OR HAVE YOUR HOMEWORK PAPER TURN INTO A CHATTERBOX AT NIGHT?

WOULD YOU RATHER THAT EVERY PIECE OF CANDY YOU TOUCH TURNS INTO BRUSSELS SPROUTS OR THAT YOUR FAVORITE TV SHOWS ARE NOW HOSTED BY VEGETABLES?

WOULD YOU RATHER FIND OUT THAT EACH TIME YOU LAUGH, YOU SOUND LIKE A DONKEY OR THAT WHEN YOU'RE TRYING TO BE SERIOUS, YOU CAN ONLY SPEAK IN SILLY RHYMES?

WOULD YOU RATHER FIND OUT THAT YOUR BED TURNS INTO A GIANT CHRISTMAS PUDDING EVERY NIGHT OR THAT YOUR PILLOW BECOMES A LAUGHING SNOWBALL?

WOULD YOU RATHER HAVE YOUR FAVORITE TOY START SINGING CHRISTMAS CAROLS NON-STOP IN JULY OR DISCOVER YOUR SCHOOL BOOKS ARE NARRATED BY RUDOLPH THE RED-NOSED REINDEER?

WOULD YOU RATHER REALIZE ALL YOUR WINTER CLOTHES HAVE TURNED INTO SANTA SUITS OR THAT YOUR WINTER BOOTS KEEP JINGLING LIKE SANTA'S SLEIGH BELLS?

WOULD YOU RATHER WAKE UP TO FIND YOUR HAIR MADE OF CANDY CANES OR THAT YOUR FINGERS HAVE TURNED INTO WIGGLY ICICLES?

WOULD YOU RATHER DISCOVER THAT YOUR BATHTUB IS FILLED WITH EGGNOG (AND YOU CAN'T DRINK IT!) OR THAT YOUR TOOTHBRUSH IS SET ON "TINSEL-CLEAN" MODE?

WOULD YOU RATHER THAT YOUR BEDROOM WALLS DISPLAY YOUR WISH LIST TO SANTA OR THAT YOUR FAVORITE CHRISTMAS COOKIE NOW ONLY RECITES "THE NIGHT BEFORE CHRISTMAS" INSTEAD OF BEING EDIBLE?

WOULD YOU RATHER FIND OUT THAT EVERY TIME YOU YAWN, SNOWFLAKES FLOAT OUT OF YOUR MOUTH OR EVERY SNEEZE SOUNDS LIKE JINGLE BELLS?

WOULD YOU RATHER HAVE YOUR CHRISTMAS STOCKING START ASKING RIDDLES BEFORE GIVING TREATS OR YOUR ADVENT CALENDAR ONLY REVEALING BRUSSELS SPROUTS?

WOULD YOU RATHER THAT EVERY CHRISTMAS ORNAMENT YOU HANG TALKS BACK (AND GIVES DECORATING TIPS) OR THAT THE CHRISTMAS TREE INSISTS ON PICKING ITS SPOT IN THE HOUSE?

WOULD YOU RATHER FIND OUT YOUR SLED HAS A MIND OF ITS OWN (AND PREFERS GOING UPHILL) OR THAT SNOWMEN YOU BUILD PLEAD FOR SUMMER VACATIONS?

WOULD YOU RATHER THAT YOUR SHADOWS TURN INTO MISCHIEVOUS ELVES OR THAT YOUR REFLECTION IN THE MIRROR ONLY APPEARS IN FESTIVE UGLY SWEATERS?

WOULD YOU RATHER FIND OUT THAT YOUR HOT CHOCOLATE CHATS ABOUT ITS DAY OR THAT YOUR CHRISTMAS CRACKERS ONLY CRACK DAD JOKES?

WOULD YOU RATHER THAT EVERY DESSERT YOU TOUCH TURNS INTO FRUITCAKE OR DISCOVER THAT A MINI SNOWSTORM FOLLOWS YOU, ENSURING YOU'RE ALWAYS WALKING IN A WINTER WONDERLAND?

WOULD YOU RATHER DISCOVER THAT YOUR ICE SKATES DEBATE ON THE BEST ICE DANCE MOVES OR THAT YOUR WINTER SCARF DEMANDS A SOLO DURING CAROL SINGING?

WOULD YOU RATHER THAT YOUR FIREPLACE INSISTS ON HEARING CHRISTMAS TALES BEFORE LIGHTING UP OR YOUR ADVENT CANDLES DEMAND A GOODNIGHT LULLABY EACH DAY?

WOULD YOU RATHER WAKE UP TO FIND ALL YOUR CHRISTMAS GIFTS EXCHANGED ROLES (YOUR NEW TOY IS NOW A FRUITCAKE AND VICE VERSA) OR THAT YOUR WINDOW VIEW IS ALWAYS A NORTH POLE SCENE?

WOULD YOU RATHER FIND OUT THAT YOUR CHRISTMAS LIGHTS PLOT TO UNTANGLE THEMSELVES OR THAT YOUR REINDEER HEADBAND THINKS IT CAN FLY?

WOULD YOU RATHER HAVE THE SNOWFLAKES NARRATE THEIR LIFE STORY AS THEY FALL OR HAVE YOUR WINTER MITTENS CHAT ABOUT THEIR SUMMER HOLIDAYS?

WOULD YOU RATHER THAT EVERY CANDY CANE YOU TOUCH TURNS INTO A CARROT OR THAT ALL YOUR WINTER MOVIES ARE NOW HOSTED BY THE ABOMINABLE SNOWMAN?

WOULD YOU RATHER FIND OUT THAT EACH TIME YOU SING A CAROL, YOU SOUND LIKE A HONKING GOOSE OR WHEN TRYING TO WHISPER TO SANTA, YOU CAN ONLY SHOUT IN FESTIVE CHEER?

Made in the USA
Las Vegas, NV
19 November 2023

81159736R00056